Little Polyglot Books

presents:

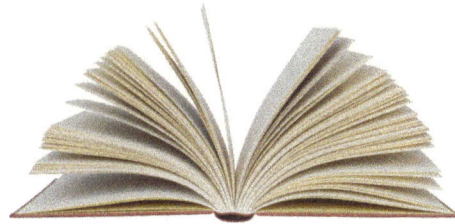

THINGS IN THE HOME

English & Yup'ik

Published by Linguacious® 2019

To Dylan and Isabella

Linguacious ®, IA, USA

www.linguacious.net

contact@linguacious.net

Little Polyglot Books - Things in the Home/Enemi Uitalriit
English & Yup'ik

www.facebook.com/linguacious

www.twitter.com/linguacious_llc

www.instagram.com/linguacious_llc

Playing the Audio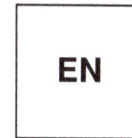

Two different ways to hear the audio for each word:

(1) Download the free Linguacious® scanner*
on your smartphone or tablet device and use it to
scan each QR code: www.linguacious.net/scanner

(2) Visit the Audio section on our
website or scan this code:

*Our scanner app is the only one that works well with our QR codes. Requires an active Internet connection.

Page Design

The language elements on each page are:

English word

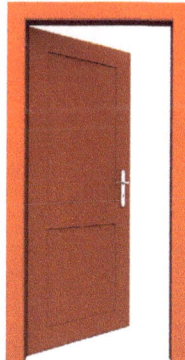

Yup'ik word

EN *black*

↑

English
QR code audio
(scan with the
Linguacious® app to hear word)

YPK *red/green/blue*

↑

Yup'ik
QR code audio
(scan with the
Linguacious® app to hear word)

backpack

atmak

2

ball

SCAN ME

SCAN ME

angqaq

3

SCAN ME

bed

SCAN ME

ingleq

book

SCAN ME

naaqerkaq

SCAN ME

SCAN ME

box

SCAN ME

yaassiik

chair

SCAN ME

SCAN ME

aqumllitaq

7

clock

SCAN ME

SCAN ME

cass'aq

8

couch

SCAN ME

aqumvik

SCAN ME

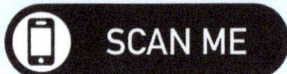
cup

caskaq

door

amiik

dress

taqmak

flower

SCAN ME

SCAN ME

naucetaaq

13

fork

kapsuun

fridge

kumlivik

15

gift

cikiun

glasses

SCAN ME

ackiik

SCAN ME

17

gloves

aliimatek

key

kelucairissuun

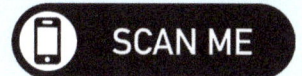

19

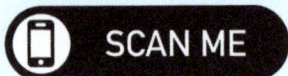

knife

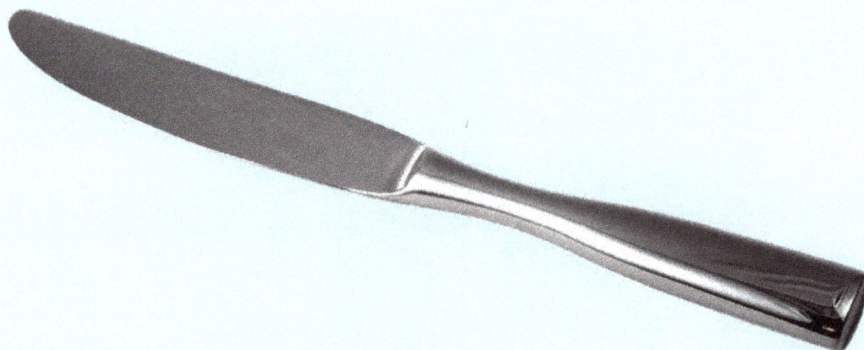

massliirissuun

20

microwave

puqlirissuun

21

SCAN ME

pants

SCAN ME

qerrulliik

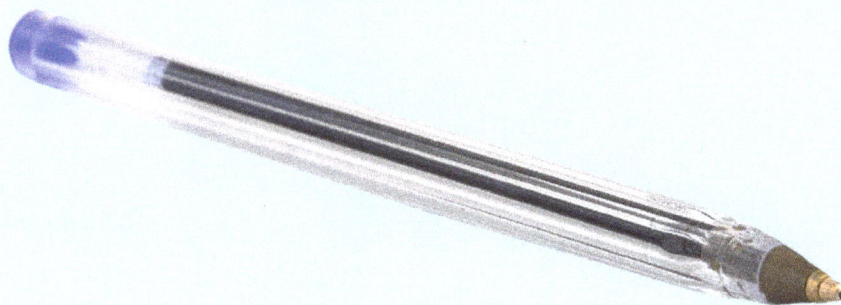

pen

igarcuun

plate

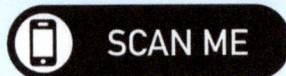
qantaq

24

scissors

SCAN ME

pupsuk

SCAN ME

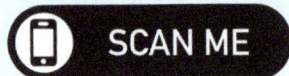
shirt

lumaraq

shoe

SCAN ME

cap'akiq

SCAN ME

sock

SCAN ME

SCAN ME

cuukiiq

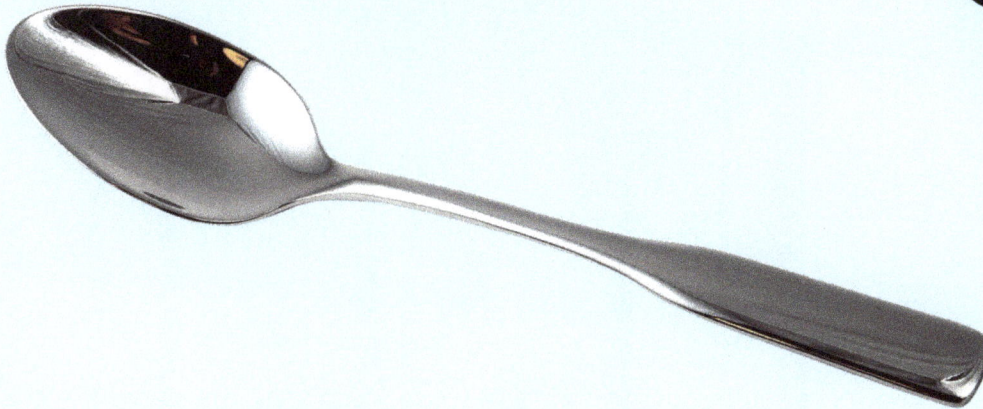

spoon

SCAN ME

SCAN ME

luuskaaq

29

table

estuuluq

television

tiiviiq

toilet

qurrun

toothbrush

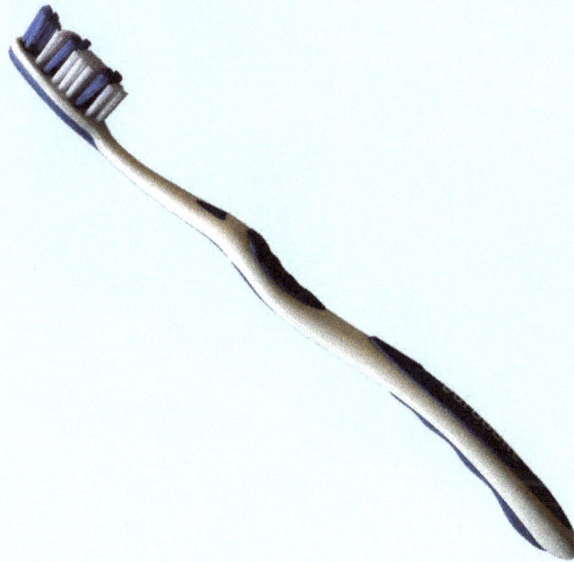

kegguciurcuun

towel

SCAN ME

SCAN ME

perriutaq

toys

naanguat

(used for three or more toys)

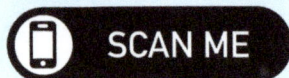
trash can

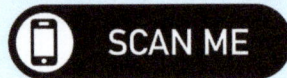
caallivik

t-shirt

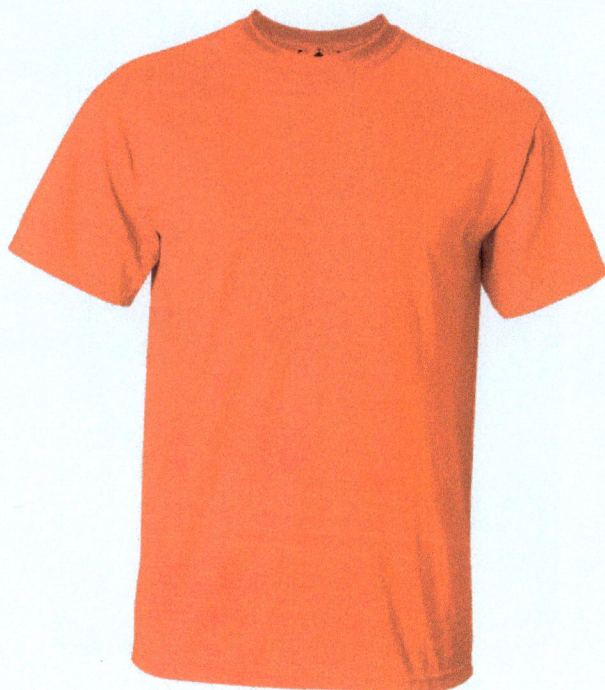

ilupeq

washing machine

iqairissuun

38

window

SCAN ME

SCAN ME

egaleq

WORD GAMES

Would you like to practice the words in this book with some free printable games?

Simply visit the link below and have fun!

www.linguacious.net/littlepolyglot-games

CPSIA information can be obtained
at www.ICGtesting.com
Printed in the USA
BVHW020116090721
611556BV00006B/26

9 781951 817343